WHAT IS THE MAGIC OF THE MAGIC

A family read-together book

DEDICATION

Being a part of a family is a learning experience, in fact the best experience ever. I have created this book during my efforts as a father and I owe all of the thanks anyone could give to my family.

by: Michael A Lambert

Pointer telling Thumb that she broke the egg.

The first finger is Pointer. Pointer can show us which direction to go or point to the subject at hand. Pointer reminds us of rule number one:

Be honest and truthful!

Tall Man helping little Merlin get up.

The second finger is Tall Man. Tall Man is the tallest of all the fingers and it gives our hand extra strength. Tall Man reminds us of rule number two:

Help those in need!

Ring Man joins his friends Pointer, Pinky, Tall Man and Thumb in their celebration.

The third finger is Ring Man which is used to show symbols of our achievements, who we love or what we believe in. Ring Man reminds us of rule number three:

Be brave and courageous!

Pinky sharing his feast with all the different friends he has made.

The fourth finger is Pinky which is the smallest of all the fingers. Pinky is used to show that we have style and class. It reminds us of rule number four:

Show tolerance!

All the friends gathered to listen to Thumb, the king.

The fifth finger is the opposable thumb. The thumb can move in the same or opposite direction of all the other fingers which helps set us apart from the other animals. Thumb reminds us of rule number five:

Be loyal to our friends and obey our leaders!

The friends realize they can accomplish even more as a team.

If we take all five fingers and get them to work together like a team; five fingers working together become ONE hand. This reminds us of rule number six:

Never boast or brag!

Together the five fingers can throw a ball, or catch it...

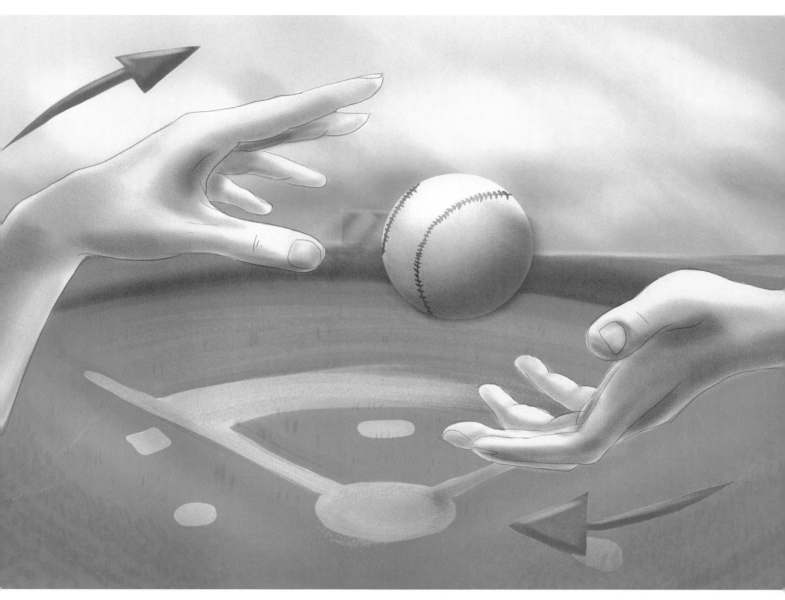

Throwing and catching a ball would be very difficult for any one of the fingers alone.

Play a musical instrument, or applaud for someone who plays one.

Whether you are the performer or clapping in the audience,
the hand plays an important part.

We can draw with our hands...

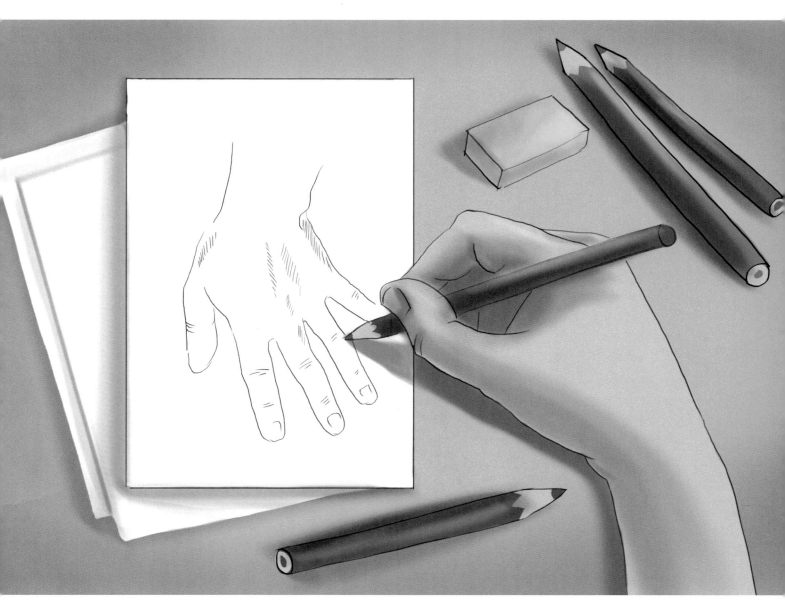

The amazing hand can even draw another hand.

and we can Shake
hands to make new
friends...

The hand can be offered as a sign of peace and friendship.

and THAT is
the magic of
the Magic Fingers!

Our performers – Pinky, Ring Man, Tall Man, Pointer and Thumb!

Acknowledgements

Design, Concepts and Story by:

Michael A Lambert

Commissioned graphic work by:

Polina Hrytskova

Editing, Proofing and other contributions

Christine Lambert

Deborah Lambert

Inspired by:

Michael C Lambert

Carol D Lambert

Made in the USA
Monee, IL
11 December 2020